NEVER LEFT

A Journey of Love, Support, and Becoming

Never Left is a journey of love, support and becoming. This story is a collection of memories meant to evoke empathy, compassion and the spirit of resilience in the reader.

Carlos wants to remind those struggling with mental health concerns to seek help, talk to a trusted family member or doctor, and know that people care.

Never Left

A Journey of Love, Support, and Becoming

Copyright © 2023
Ablavi L. de Souza
King-David Hughton

All rights reserved. No portion of this book may be reproduced, republished, broadcasted, adapted, transmitted in any form, or stored in any system without permission from the publisher except as permitted by Canadian copyright law.

Published by
Hughton Books and Publishers
www.hughtonbooks.com

ISBN: 978-1-7386309-8-1

Printed in the U.S.A.

Hughton Books
&
PUBLISHERS

"So, Mom, I just wanted to say it clearly:
I am

Carlos!

And I am here to stay!
Yeap!
Thanks for taking care of me, Mom!"

"You are welcome, Carlos! Remember, I am always here for you, son! Stay true to yourself, be kind to others, and never lose sight of the kind and loving person you are."

"Thank you, Mom! You never stop saying nice words to me. I remember the many times you have said those lovely words to me.

"I will always be here for you!"

You never left me to go away. Nope, not at all! You have always stayed by my side.

You are like a star
that brightens my day!"

"So are you, Carlos! You are my superstar, and you're forever loved!"

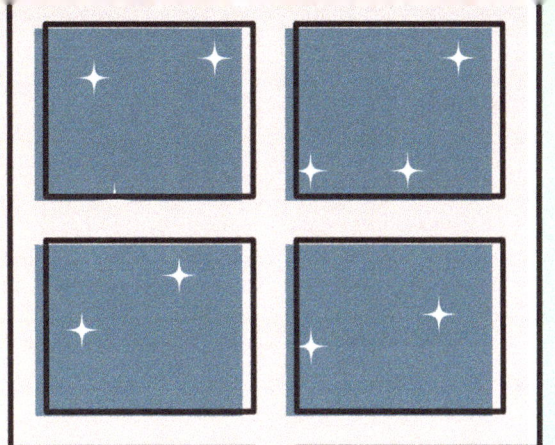

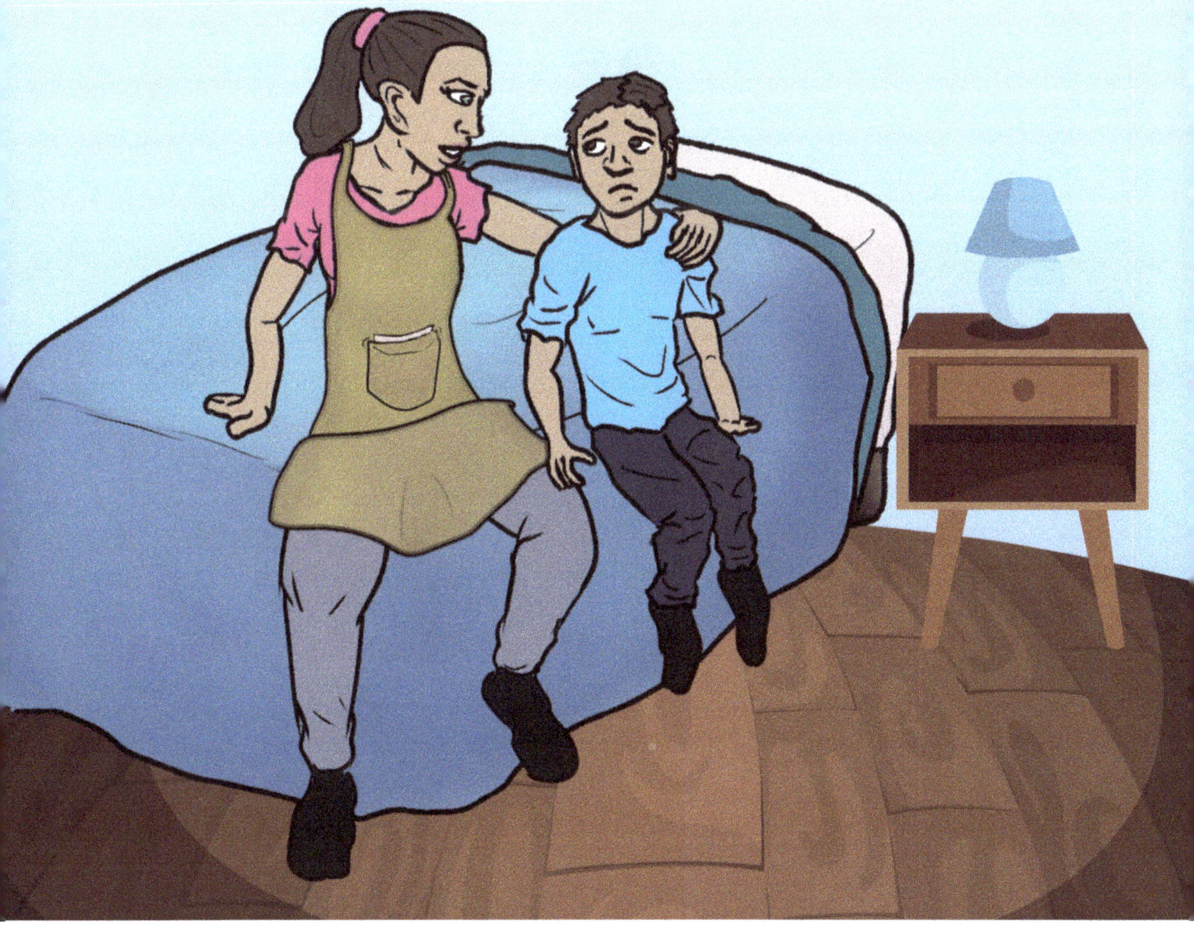

"Mom. Do you remember the first week of school last year? I missed a whole week of school because I did not feel too well.
After we returned from the clinic, you became a superhero nurse like the ones on TV. You took my temperature daily, gave me medicine, cooked up grandma's special chicken soup, and kept checking on me to ensure I was all right!"

"Mom. Do you also remember the day I turned the living room walls into a large piece of paper and drew Blue Mountains?"

"You have such a good memory, Carlos!"

"Sometimes I forget some things, but I also remember many things, Mom."

"That is why you are my superstar, son!"

"Thanks, Mom!
Dad looked surprised the day I drew the blue mountains on the walls. But he never left. I was happy that you both helped me clean the walls."

"This next memory is like a treasure to me. Remember when you took me to the community swimming pool to learn how to swim?

I was scared to jump into the water. But guess what? You never left, Mom. You said something nice to me that day."

"What did I say, Carlos?"

"You said
I can sit and watch the other kids or go home and come back whenever I am ready."

"What a great mom you are!

I remember the day you surprised me with a shiny new bicycle that looked like the fastest motorbike ever! You wanted me to ride the bike across the world, but I was wobbly and could not quite do it. But you know what?

You never left!

Not even for a second! You were right there, helping me and encouraging me to keep trying."

"Mom, do you remember the day my teacher told you I was drawing geese on the math quiz?"

"How could I ever forget that, Carlos?"

"That was silly of me!
But guess what?

My teacher stayed!

Neither did she get upset. She kept checking on me and reminding me to stay focused so I could do better."

"You are a brave boy, Carlos!"

"Thanks, Mom! I am brave because you taught me to talk about things that happen to me.

Here comes another one. Do you recall that day at the playground when I told you I saw many birds flying around? It was like a magical bird party!

Unfortunately, my friends could not see the birds but never left me. Yes, Mom. They never stopped being my friends. They have been
magnificent friends!"

"Remember that stormy December evening when our family had a yummy dinner with Grandma, Aunty Maria, and my big cousins?
I could not socialize or chat with them.
But guess what?

The family never left or forgot about me.

After they returned, they kept calling to ensure I was okay."

"Mom. Remember last year when I could not dress myself up for some days?
You did not know what was happening.

Guess what? You never left me with my struggle. Nope! Not at all!

Each time I could not get myself dressed, you helped me get all dressed up!
You are a good mother, Mom!"

"You are priceless, Carlos!"

"I remember that final week of summer when I had trouble sleeping last year.
You started preparing calming baths for me, and during the nights, you stayed by my side, helping me breathe in and out. Then you'll carefully cover me in my favourite blue blankets.

Thanks, Mom!"

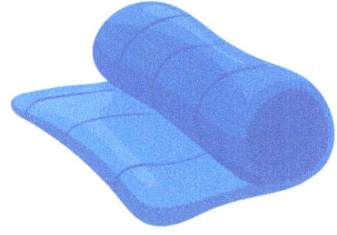

"You're welcome, Carlos!"

"Here is another crucial memory, Mom.

I remember when you returned from visiting Aunty Maria in Ecuador. You looked at me carefully and said,

"You are not feeling well, my child."

You seemed worried, but you never left. You stayed with me and took me to different appointments so I could get help for my anxiety."

"You have always protected me, Mom! When the doctor called you about my health, you said,

"Oh, now I understand."

You never left!

With tears of joy, it's like you wrapped me up in your love and made everything feel better!"

"I know I have made you go through happy and challenging times. You will cherish and treasure these times because, in my struggle, you never left!

And like a mother full of hope, you never gave up on me!"

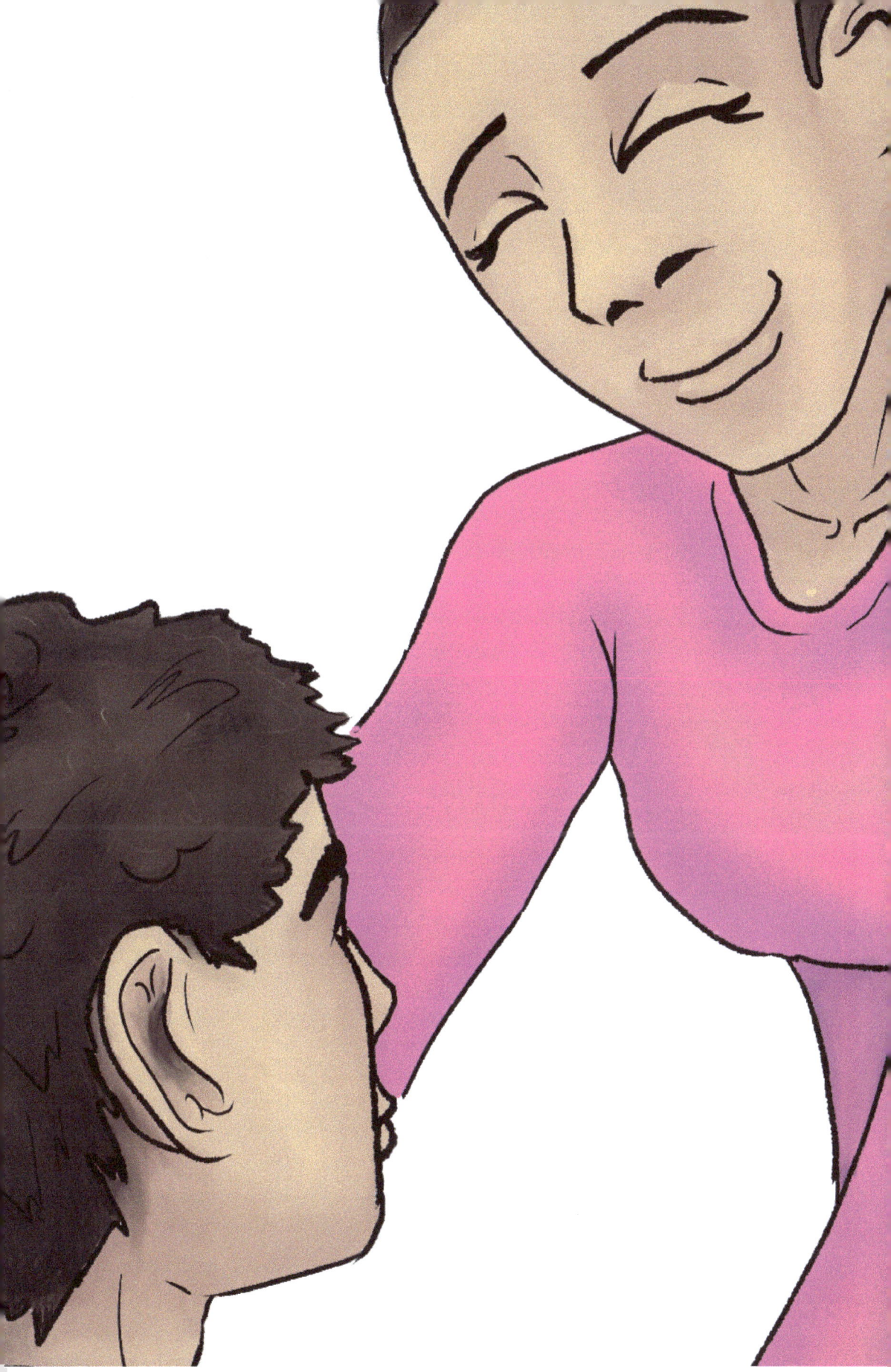

"YES!

Your love never ends, Mom.

You, Dad, my friends, Grandma, Grandpa, Aunties, Uncles, cousins, teachers, doctors, and the universe! You all believed in my strength and my potential.

So, you never left! You always stayed!"

"And like a shining star, we keep shining brighter and brighter than we can imagine—all of us together.

Whether my body is strong or not, we make a strong team, just like superheroes with capes, because you never left!"

The End

Ablavi L. De Souza is an author of children's books. Outside her work of authorship, Ms. De Souza is an educator and the founder of the non-profit organization AfriCanada Hub. She seeks creative ways to bridge educational gaps between children from marginalized communities and their counterparts. Her work in the community has been characterized by an adept love of reading children's books with children and to children. Outside her professional life, Ms. de Souza loves to pray, watch movies, drink tea, and try out new recipes.

Author

KingDavid Hughton is a true artist, excelling not only as a concept artist and illustrator but also as a dedicated student.

Drawing and making artistic work is integral to who he is - a passionate calling that flows through his very being. When he's not immersed in school or his artwork, you'll find him writing stories, sharing vibrant moments playing video games with friends, going for walks, or enjoying his other passion - cooking in the kitchen.

Illustrator

www.ingramcontent.com/pod-product-compliance
Lightning Source LLC
Chambersburg PA
CBHW050805220426
43209CB00088BA/1646